Advent and Christmas Wisdom
from
SAINT ALPHONSUS LIGUORI

Advent and Christmas Wisdom

from

SAINT ALPHONSUS LIGUORI

Daily Scripture and Prayers Together
With Saint Alphonsus Liguori's Own Words

Compiled by Maurice J. Nutt, CSsR

Liguori
LIGUORI, MISSOURI

Imprimi Potest: Harry Grile, CSsR
Provincial, Denver Province, The Redemptorists

Published by Liguori Publications
Liguori, Missouri 63057

To order, call 800-325-9521
www.liguori.org

Library of Congress Cataloging-in-Publication Data

Liguori, Alfonso Maria de', Saint, 1696–1787.
[Selections. English. 2011]
Advent and Christmas wisdom from Saint Alphonsus Liguori: daily Scripture and prayers together with Saint Alphonsus Liguori's own words / compiled by Maurice J. Nutt.—1st ed.

p. cm.

ISBN 978-0-7648-1909-4
1. Advent—Prayers and devotions. 2. Christmas—Prayers and devotions. 3. Catholic Church—Prayers and devotions. I. Nutt, Maurice J. II. Title.
BX2170.A4L5413 2011
242'.33—dc22

2011006554

Liguori Publications, a nonprofit corporation, is an apostolate of the Redemptorists. To learn more about the Redemptorists, visit Redemptorists.com.

Printed in the United States of America
15 14 13 12 11 / 5 4 3 2 1
First Edition

Contents

Introduction

It has been said that when one reads the writings of Saint Alphonsus Liguori, it is as though a person is listening in on a very intimate conversation between Saint Alphonsus and the saints. A very holy man himself, Saint Alphonsus Liguori, in his characteristic self-effacing humility, almost always defers to the wisdom and sanctity of other holy men and women of the Church.

Saint Alphonsus Liguori is credited with writing over one hundred books. This prolific writer entertained subjects from prayer to preaching, from the Blessed Virgin Mary to moral theology, from the practice of the love of Jesus Christ to the preparation for death, and from the duties and dignity of the priesthood to the responsibilities of vowed religious. While his vast and expansive literary career covered many themes and topics, a few were constant. He was endeared to the Incarnation, the Passion, the Eucharist, and to the Blessed Virgin Mary. Besides being an ardent devotee to Mary, his spirituality was grounded in the "crib, cross, and Sacrament."

Appreciating Saint Alphonsus Liguori is an acquired taste, for he was not a man of apparitions or flamboyant religiosity. While in many ways a brilliant man—possessing a genius intellect and a connoisseur of culture, music, and art—he was an ordinary man who understood deeply the phenomenal love of God for all humanity. It was the presence of this love in his life that allowed him to realize that every person mattered—they mattered to God, and they mattered to him.

His incessant desire to love Jesus above all things urged Alphonsus to ponder in his writings, preaching, and music the unfathomable doctrine of the Incarnation. How could God love us so much that he would send his only-begotten Son into our world as a small infant? And as if that wasn't enough, Alphonsus marveled at God's entering as a babe born in the midst of a filthy, smelly animal stable. Saint Alphonsus often decried the fact that God loved us so much that he allowed his Son to be born for our salvation in subhuman conditions, and yet the world neglected, rejected, and ultimately crucified him.

Saint Alphonsus Liguori often lamented that God loved us too much and we loved God too little. Yet Alphonsus was convinced that anyone who looked upon a Nativity scene at Christmastime and gazed upon the face of the Infant Jesus would see love incarnate and come to know and love God.

In addition to his insistence that all would come to love God through contemplation on the Babe of Bethlehem, Saint Alphonsus Liguori sought to bring the Good News of the Incarnation in song. This method of catechizing and evangelizing through song was especially effective among the unlearned and the poor. He would either use common melodies of his time and Neapolitan culture or create original songs and music that were both moving and memorable. The most famous and widely celebrated Christmas carol in Italy even today is *"Tu Scendi Dalle Stelle, O Re del Cielo"* ("You Came Down From the Stars, O King of Heaven"), composed by Saint Alphonsus Liguori in 1755 while staying at the Convent of the Consolation, one of the Redemptorist houses in the small city of Deliceto, in southeastern Italy. While Saint Alphonsus Liguori certainly sings of the Christmas mystery, his ultimate intent was to invite Christians to enter into that mystery. The renowned composer Giuseppi Verdi once commented, "Without this song by Saint Alphonsus Liguori, Christmas isn't Christmas."

Alphonsus Mary Anthony John Francis Cosmas Damian Michael Gaspar de' Liguori was born the eldest of eight children in his father's country house at Marianella, near Naples, on September 27, 1696. The choice of many names is easily explained. Alphonsus was a traditional Liguori family name, while Cosmas, Damian, and the Archangel Michael were the liturgical patrons of the days of his birth and baptism; Mary was reflective of his mother's love of the Blessed Virgin, Anthony and Francis were from his mother's devotion to these saints and her education by the Franciscan nuns.

At the age of sixteen, Alphonsus received a double doctorate in both civil and church law from the University of Naples. He practiced law before the courts of Naples for several years. Undoubtedly the youngest lawyer in the Neapolitan Bar, he was a successful and popular attorney who was noted never to have lost a case. However, in 1723 Alphonsus argued a case that would ultimately be his last. God's will for Alphonsus was to become a priest. Alphonsus left his law profession and spent days in prayer, seeking to know God's will.

On December 21, 1726, at the age of thirty, Alphonsus was ordained to the priesthood. For six years he labored in and around Naples, giving missions, ministering to the incurables, visiting prisoners, and preaching to the poor street people. He trained lay catechists who would then work in the slums, and he himself went into the slums to address the spiritual abandonment he found there. It was this initial encounter with the abandoned poor that God used to call Alphonsus to his lifework.

In 1732, Alphonsus Liguori founded a religious congregation in the mountain region of Scala, near Amalfi. He and his companions preached to the poor goatherds who were spiritually abandoned. This little band of missionaries grew to be the Congregation of the Most Holy Redeemer, known the world over as the Redemptorists.

Today this humble man who deeply loved the Infant Jesus is recognized as a doctor of the Church and the patron saint of confessors, moral theologians, and those suffering from arthritis. Saint Alphonsus Liguori's life could be summed up as one of Advent waiting. He never sought to get ahead of God's will but was content with waiting. Saint Alphonsus' waiting was not idle waiting but expectant waiting. He believed God's revelations were true and to be trusted. As you journey with Saint Alphonsus Liguori throughout the Advent and Christmas seasons, may you come to love the Babe of Bethlehem and make a suitable dwelling place for him in your heart.

How to Use This Book

Advent—that period of great anticipatory joy—is a time of preparation for the celebration of Christ's arrival in Bethlehem as a helpless infant. In the Western liturgy, Advent begins four Sundays prior to December 25—the Sunday closest to November 30, which is the feast of Saint Andrew, one of Jesus' first disciples.

The annual commemoration of Christ's birth begins the Christmas cycle of the liturgical year—a cycle that runs from Christmas day to the Baptism of the Lord. In keeping with the unfolding of the message of the liturgical year, this book is designed to be used from the first Sunday of Advent through twelve days of the Christmas cycle, or until January 6.

The four weeks of Advent are often thought of as symbolizing the four different ways Christ comes into the world: (1) upon his birth as a helpless infant; (2) upon his arrival in the hearts of believers; (3) upon his death; and (4) upon his arrival on Judgment Day.

Because Christmas falls on a different day of the week each year, the fourth week of Advent is never really finished; it is abruptly, joyously, and solemnly abrogated by the annual coming again of Christ at Christmas. Christ's Second Coming will also one day abruptly interrupt our sojourn here on Earth.

Since the calendar dictates the number of days in Advent, this book includes Scripture quotations and meditative excerpts from the writings of Saint Alphonsus Liguori for twenty-eight days. These daily readings make up Part I; on Christmas day the book switches to Part II, which contains materials for twelve days of the Christmas season. If Part I contains any "extra" entries, these may be read by doubling up on days or by reading two entries on weekends. Or one may just skip those entries that do not fit within the Advent time frame of a particular year.

Each "day" in this book begins with the words of Saint Alphonsus Liguori. Following that quotation is an excerpt from Scripture that is related in some way. Next is a prayer, also built on the ideas from the two preceding passages. Finally, an Advent or Christmas "action" suggests ways in which to apply the messages to one's daily life.

Part III proposes two optional formats for using each day as part of a longer liturgical observance similar to Night Prayer, combined with a version of the Office of Readings. These options are for those who may wish to use this book as part of a more developed individual or group observance. The purpose of these readings is to enrich the Advent/Christmas/Epiphany season of the liturgical year and set up a means by which individuals, families, or groups can observe the true meaning of the season.

PART I

~

READINGS *for* ADVENT

DAY 1

The Redeeming Plan

*C*onsider how God allowed 4,000 years to pass after the sin of Adam before he sent his Son on earth to redeem the world. And in the meantime, what fatal darkness reigned on the earth! The true God was not known or adored, except in one small corner of the world. Idolatry reigned everywhere; devils and beasts and stones were adored as gods....If Jesus Christ had come into the world immediately after the Fall of Adam, the greatness of this favor would have been but slightly appreciated. Let us, therefore, thank the goodness of God for having sent us into the world after the great work of redemption was accomplished.

THE INCARNATION, BIRTH AND INFANCY OF JESUS CHRIST

SCRIPTURE

The days are coming—oracle of the LORD—when I will fulfill
the promise made to the house of Israel and the house of Judah.
In those days, at that time, I will make a just shoot spring up for
David; he shall do what is right and just in the land. In those
days Judah shall be saved and Jerusalem shall dwell safely; this
is the name they shall call her: "The LORD our justice."

JEREMIAH 33:14–16

PRAYER

Creator and creating God, you give me such a delightful and
wholesome gift in a new beginning. Pride, rebellion, and
temptation called to me, and I pulled away from you. These
identical issues continue to cause sin in the lives of your
people. Rather than true confession, like the first Adam, I seek
to blame others for the troubles in my life. Forgive me of my
sins. Allow me to begin this Advent sojourn by restoring me
to a fresh start and new beginning with and in you. Amen.

ADVENT ACTION

Whatever is at the center of your life will be the source of
your security, peace, wisdom, and power. Decide today to
make Jesus the center and source of everything in your life.

DAY 2

Fullness of Grace

$\mathcal{B}$ehold the happy time is come which was called the designated time: "When the designated time had come, God sent his Son…to deliver from the law those who were subjected to it" (Gal 4:4). It is called the fullness of time because of the fullness of grace which the Son of God came to communicate to [us] by the redemption of the world.

The Incarnation, Birth and Infancy of Jesus Christ

SCRIPTURE

Brothers [and sisters]: May the Lord make you increase and abound in love for one another and for all, just as we have for you, so as to strengthen your hearts, to be blameless in holiness before our God and Father at the coming of our Lord Jesus with all his holy ones. [Amen.]

Finally, brothers [and sisters], we earnestly ask and exhort you in the Lord Jesus that, as you received from us how you should conduct yourselves to please God—and as you are conducting yourselves—you do so even more. For you know what instructions we gave you through the Lord Jesus.

1 THESSALONIANS 3:12—4:2

PRAYER

Lord, it is my hope that I may always be in "your will and way." Sometimes I am selfish with my time and my own desires. Today, help me sort out things in my life. I need to make you the first priority in my life and not the things that really do not matter. Assist me in conducting myself in ways that are most pleasing to you. Lord, it is my desire to live more for you this day. Amen.

ADVENT ACTION

Advent is a time to practice patience. Today, be patient with yourself and those around you. Spiritual growth is tender; it's holy ground. There's simply no greater investment.

DAY 3

No Doubt About God's Love

*P*rior to the Incarnation of Jesus we might have doubted whether God loved us so much. But after the birth, life, and death of Jesus, how can we have any doubt whatsoever that God loves us with the most tender love? What greater love could God show us than to sacrifice his divine Son for love of us?

PREPARATION FOR DEATH

SCRIPTURE

Beloved, let us love one another, because love is of God; everyone who loves is begotten by God and knows God. Whoever is without love does not know God, for God is love. In this way the love of God was revealed to us: God sent his only Son into the world so that we might have life through him. In this is love: not that we have loved God, but that he loved us and sent his Son as expiation for our sins. Beloved, if God so loved us, we also must love one another. No one has ever seen God. Yet, if we love one another, God remains in us, and his love is brought to perfection in us.

1 JOHN 4:7–12

PRAYER

Good and gracious God, I sincerely thank and praise you for loving me. Your love is the joy of my life. Lord, help me to love you and others totally. Take away any malice or bitterness in my life. Help me love as your Son, Jesus, loved. I resolve to bless and pray for those who persecute me—who are cruel in their attitude toward me. I bless them and do not curse them. Therefore, allow love and kindness to shine forth in my life. Let others witness the love of Christ in my life in all I say and do. Lord, be glorified in my life today. Amen.

ADVENT ACTION

Without involvement, there is no real commitment. Today, resolve to become involved and committed to something or someone in need of your time, your talents, or your presence.

DAY 4

Mary's "Yes"

*P*icture the angel who is sent as ambassador into the town of Nazareth to announce to the Virgin Mary the coming of the Word who desires to become incarnate in her womb. The angel salutes her, calls her full of grace and blessed among women. The humble Virgin, chosen to be the Mother of the Son of God, is troubled at these praises because of her great humility. But the angel encourages her, and tells her that she has found grace with God, the grace which brought peace between God and [humanity] and the reparation of the ruin caused by sin. He then tells her that she must give her Son the name of Savior—"You shall give him the name Jesus"—and that this, her Son, is the very Son of God who is to redeem the world and thus to reign over the hearts of [all].

THE INCARNATION, BIRTH AND INFANCY OF JESUS CHRIST

SCRIPTURE

In the sixth month, the angel Gabriel was sent from God to a town of Galilee called Nazareth, to a virgin betrothed to a man named Joseph, of the house of David, and the virgin's name was Mary. And coming to her, he said, "Hail, favored one! The Lord is with you." But she was greatly troubled at what was said and pondered what sort of greeting this might be. Then the angel said to her, "Do not be afraid, Mary, for you have found favor with God. Behold, you will conceive in your womb and bear a son, and you shall name him Jesus. He will be great and will be called Son of the Most High, and the Lord God will give him the throne of David his father, and he will rule over the house of Jacob forever, and of his kingdom there will be no end."

But Mary said to the angel, "How can this be, since I have no relations with a man?"

And the angel said to her in reply, "The holy Spirit will come upon you, and the power of the Most High will overshadow you. Therefore the child to be born will be called holy, the Son of God. And behold, Elizabeth, your relative, has also conceived a son in her old age, and this is the sixth month for her who was called barren; for nothing will be impossible for God."

Mary said, "Behold, I am the handmaid of the Lord. May it be done to me according to your word." Then the angel departed from her.

LUKE 1:26–38

PRAYER

Loving God, as the Word made flesh, your Son, Jesus, came to an unprepared people in an unprepared place. In this Advent time and space, I realize just how unprepared I am to welcome your darling Son. Lord, instill in me a spirit of urgency to "get ready," to stop making excuses, to stop "messing around," to make my life ready and acceptable to the Lord. Prepare my soul to welcome my most precious Soul Mate. Order my steps in your Word so that all you have prepared for me may be done according to your Word. Blessed Mother, I seek your intercession. Amen.

ADVENT ACTION

Today, take some time to note some of your good qualities. Write down these qualities and meditate on them throughout the day. Like Mary, trust and praise God for the Holy Spirit's "overshadowing" your life.

DAY 5

The Word Is God

The eternal Word descends on earth to save [humanity]; and from where does he descend? "At one end of the heavens it comes forth" (Ps 19:7). He descends from the bosom of his divine Father, where from eternity he was begotten in the brightness of sanctity. And where does he descend? He descends into the womb of a Virgin, a child of Adam, which in comparison with the bosom of God is an object of horror. Therefore, the Church sings, "You did not abhor the Virgin's womb." Yes, because the Word is God, he is immense, omnipotent, most blessed, and supreme Lord, and equal in everything to the Father.

THE INCARNATION, BIRTH AND INFANCY OF JESUS CHRIST

SCRIPTURE

In the beginning was the Word, and the Word was with God, and the Word was God. He was in the beginning with God. All things came to be through him, and without him nothing came to be. What came to be through him was life, and this life was the light of the human race; the light shines in the darkness, and the darkness has not overcome it.

JOHN 1:1–5

PRAYER

O God, your Word is a lamp unto my feet and a light to my path. Guide my feet, Lord, lest I stumble on my Advent journey. May I be encouraged to study your Word, believe your Word, and follow your Word as I strive to grow closer to you and your holy Word. Enable me to speak and share your Word so your Word will indeed go forth and do the work it is purposed to do and not return to me void. Let your Word become a part of me so that I may be a worthy Word-bearer and Word-sharer to all I meet this day. Use me to light a darkened path in the world today. Amen.

ADVENT ACTION

Today, set aside one hour to study sacred Scripture. Perhaps you may want to study more in-depth the Scripture citation for today or some other Scripture text. Seek God deeply today in the study of God's Word. How is God's Word speaking to you within the context of your life's circumstances?

DAY 6

No Better Medicine

*F*ive hundred years before Christ was born, the priest-prophet Zechariah looked ahead into the coming centuries and foretold: *When that day comes, clansmen of David and citizens of Jerusalem shall have a free-flowing fountain in which the sinner will be cleansed.* The Blessed Sacrament is the flowing fountain the prophet foresaw. It flows freely so that those who wish can wash away the stains of sin that spot their souls each day. For our daily faults and failings, there is no better medicine than to come to the Blessed Sacrament.

VISITS TO THE MOST BLESSED SACRAMENT
AND THE BLESSED VIRGIN MARY

SCRIPTURE

[Brothers and sisters:] I give thanks to my God at every remembrance of you, praying always with joy in my every prayer for all of you, because of your partnership for the gospel from the first day until now. I am confident of this, that the one who began a good work in you will continue to complete it until the day of Christ Jesus....For God is my witness, how I long for all of you with the affection of Christ Jesus. And this is my prayer: that your love may increase ever more and more in knowledge and every kind of perception, to discern what is of value, so that you may be pure and blameless for the day of Christ, filled with the fruit of righteousness that comes through Jesus Christ for the glory and praise of God.

PHILIPPIANS 1:4–6, 8–11

PRAYER

Omnipresent God, stop me, still me, enfold me so that I may be fully aware of your divine presence. You are always around me, with me, and within me, but too often I take your presence for granted. Forgive me, Lord, for my lack of awareness and respect for your presence and working in my life. I stop to acknowledge today that you are the source and sustenance of my very being. I honor and praise you today for making me who I am and awakening me to whose I am. With a grateful heart, I claim this all in Jesus' name. Amen.

ADVENT ACTION

Saint Alphonsus marveled at how Jesus made himself always present and available for us in the Blessed Sacrament. Today, make an effort to be sensitive to the loneliness of others, and make an effort to be "present" to them; be a sacramental sign of Christ's presence in the midst of their loneliness.

DAY 7

Confidence in God

In rising from bed, St. Philip Neri used to say every morning: O Lord, keep thy hand this day over Philip; if thou do not, Philip will betray thee. And one day, as he walked through the city, reflecting on his own misery, he frequently said, *I despair, I despair.* A certain religious who heard him, believing that the saint was really tempted to despair, corrected him, and encouraged him to hope in the divine mercy. But the saint replied: "I despair of myself, but I trust in God." Therefore, during this life, in which we are exposed to so many dangers of losing God, it is necessary for us to live always in great diffidence of ourselves, and full of confidence in God.

THE SERMONS OF ST. ALPHONSUS LIGUORI

SCRIPTURE

[After the man, Adam, had eaten of the tree] The LORD God then called to the man and asked him: Where are you? He answered, "I heard you in the garden; but I was afraid, because I was naked, so I hid." Then God asked: Who told you that you were naked? Have you eaten from the tree of which I had forbidden you to eat?

The man replied, "The woman whom you put here with me—she gave me fruit from the tree, so I ate it." The LORD God then asked the woman: What is this you have done? The woman answered, "The snake tricked me, so I ate it."

Then the LORD God said to the snake: Because you have done this, cursed are you among all the animals, tame or wild; on your belly you shall crawl, and dust you shall eat all the days of your life. I will put enmity between you and the woman, and between your offspring and hers; they will strike at your head, while you strike at their heel....

The man gave his wife the name "Eve," because she was the mother of all the living.

GENESIS 3:9–15, 20

PRAYER

Dear Lord, Saint Philip Neri's prayer could very well be my prayer. I need you to keep your hand on me. If you withdraw your hand from me, I would draw away from you. Lord, never let me be separated from you. I trust in you with full confidence to guide and protect me from all that leads me into temptation and sin. Lord, I am nothing without you. Be my help and defense, especially when I find myself in times of trouble. Amen.

ADVENT ACTION

Today, if there is anyone with whom you've had an argument or serious disagreement, make every effort to restore peace to that broken relationship.

DAY 8

A Pattern for Sanctity

*M*any try to devise their own pattern for sanctity. If they are introverts, they say that sanctity consists in living in seclusion. If they are extroverts, they say that holiness consists in preaching and argumentation. If they are naturally generous, they argue that sanctity is attained only by giving money to the poor. Such actions are the fruit of the love of Jesus Christ; but love itself consists in complete union with the will of God. And in order to do this, we must deny ourselves and prefer to do what is pleasing to God.

THE PRACTICE OF THE LOVE OF JESUS CHRIST

SCRIPTURE

Jesus said to the crowds: "Come to me, all you who labor and are burdened, and I will give you rest. Take my yoke upon you and learn from me, for I am meek and humble of heart; and you will find rest for yourselves. For my yoke is easy, and my burden light."

MATTHEW 11:28–30

PRAYER

Merciful God, bless me as I go about my daily life and sometimes experience disappointments, regrets, burdens, and misunderstandings. Bless me to become more sensitive in my communication so that I avoid giving mixed and confusing messages. Guard my tongue so that it may be a faithful tool of love and justice, not the source of scorn and hate. Sometimes when I am unhappy or hurting, Lord, I tend to hurt others. Allow me to love the "God in me" so that I can love the "God in others." Share my burdens, Lord, so that I won't be a burden to others. Amen.

ADVENT ACTION

Today, let go of some past hurt and pray for the person who has caused you pain.

DAY 9

Not Happy
Without Redeeming Us

*C*onsider that the eternal Word is that God who is so infinitely happy in himself that his happiness cannot be greater than it is, nor could the salvation of all [humankind] have added anything to it or have diminished it.

THE INCARNATION, BIRTH AND INFANCY OF JESUS CHRIST

SCRIPTURE

[Brothers and sisters:] Blessed be the God and Father of our Lord Jesus Christ, who has blessed us in Christ with every spiritual blessing in the heavens, as he chose us in him, before the foundation of the world, to be holy and without blemish before him. In

love he destined us for adoption to himself through Jesus Christ, in accord with the favor of his will, for the praise of the glory of his grace that he granted us in the beloved.

In him we were also chosen, destined in accord with the purpose of the One who accomplishes all things according to the intention of his will, so that we might exist for the praise of his glory, we who first hoped in Christ.

EPHESIANS 1:3–6, 11–12

PRAYER

O God, waiting without hope is torture. Waiting without help produces fear. My hope is in you, my God, who is "an ever-present help in time of trouble." I claim my place and position as a "child of God." As I await with great expectation the coming of Jesus in this Advent season, I expect and prepare for great things and put aside majoring in minor issues that really don't matter. I accept the call to live for Christ and will seek to avoid the obstacles that lead me into evil. Help me, Lord Jesus, as I await your coming. Amen.

ADVENT ACTION

Today, spend a half-hour in total silence and passively observe and note the people and things that float before your mind's eye. Pray for the people and things that result from this moment of meditation.

DAY 10

A Gift of Love

A devout author says that if Jesus Christ had permitted us to ask him to give us the greatest proof of his love, who would have ventured to ask of him that he should become a child like us, that he should clothe himself with all our miseries, and make himself, of all men, the most poor, the most despised, and the most ill-treated?

THE INCARNATION, BIRTH AND INFANCY OF JESUS CHRIST

SCRIPTURE

Shout for joy, daughter Zion! sing joyfully, Israel! Be glad and exult with all your heart, daughter Jerusalem! The LORD has removed the judgment against you, he has turned away your enemies; the King of Israel, the LORD, is in your midst, you have no further misfortune to fear. On that day, it shall be said to Jerusalem: Do not fear, Zion, do not be discouraged! The LORD, your God, is in your midst, a mighty savior, who will rejoice over you with gladness, and renew you in his love, who will sing joyfully because of you, as on festival days.

ZEPHANIAH 3:14–18A

PRAYER

I give thanks this day for the gifts of a loving God. I rejoice that when I forgot God at times, God, in covenantal love, did not forget me: I am so grateful. Let me never be torn from you, gracious One. Lord, I desire to love you with my whole heart. Your love for me is so faithful and enduring. Even when I sin and fall short, you continue to love and uphold me. I thank and praise you for your grace and mercy in my life. Yes, I am so grateful. Amen.

ADVENT ACTION

Today, take some time to remember the changes you have gone through up to this point in your life. Remember that even in those most difficult times, God was present with you. Thank God today for his ever-abiding presence in your life.

DAY 11

Hope in God Strengthens Us

*T*he prophet Isaiah says, "They that hope in the Lord shall renew their strength; they shall take wings as eagles; they shall run, and not be weary; they shall walk, and not grow faint" (Is 40:31). They who place their confidence in God shall renew their strength; they shall lay aside their own weakness, and shall acquire the strength of God; they shall fly like eagles in the way of the Lord, without fatigue and without ever failing.... [The person] who hopes in the Lord shall be encompassed by his mercy, so that he [or she] shall never be abandoned by it.

THE SERMONS OF ST. ALPHONSUS LIGUORI

SCRIPTURE

[Brothers and sisters:] Rejoice in the Lord always. I shall say it again: rejoice! Your kindness should be known to all. The Lord is near. Have no anxiety at all, but in everything, by prayer and petition, with thanksgiving, make your requests known to God. Then the peace of God that surpasses all understanding will guard your hearts and minds in Christ Jesus.

PHILIPPIANS 4:4–7

PRAYER

O life-giving God, I thank you for lifting my woeful spirit and filling the void in my heart with your holy presence. When I feel alone and empty, Lord, let me always feel your all-powerful presence within me and surrounding me, filling me with life anew. In Jesus' name, I pray. Amen.

ADVENT ACTION

Select your words with care today, opting for silence rather than being harsh and insensitive. Act with empathy today, and make every effort to affirm and support your friends and loved ones.

DAY 12

Resolving to Love God

*L*ord, you love us too much. There is nothing more you can do to make us love you. How unreasonable we are if our love is cool and distant. Give us the strength to love you intensely! Draw us gently to your love. Make us see the great claim you have on our affection....I love you, my Jesus. You alone are my Treasure; you alone can satisfy me; you alone are my Love. You have spent yourself lavishly for me. Now I must live my life for you.

VISITS TO THE MOST BLESSED SACRAMENT

AND THE BLESSED VIRGIN MARY

SCRIPTURE

I love the LORD, who listened to my voice in supplication, who turned an ear to me on the day I called. I was caught by the cords of death; the snares of Sheol had seized me; I felt agony and dread. Then I called on the name of the LORD, "O LORD, save my life!"

Gracious is the LORD and righteous; yes, our God is merciful. The LORD protects the simple; I was helpless, but he saved me. Return, my soul, to your rest; the LORD has been very good to you. For my soul has been freed from death, my eyes from tears, my feet from stumbling. I shall walk before the LORD in the land of the living.

PSALM 116:1–9

PRAYER

Jesus, you are the center of my joy. You have called me into a beautiful love relationship. You invite me to love you and my brothers and sisters. And yet I have failed to obey your law and have rejected your invitation to love. In my desire to live the "good life," I have become inwardly focused. I have neglected the care of others and have not loved my neighbor as I love myself. Forgive me and restore in me a true spirit of love. Amen.

ADVENT ACTION

Saint Alphonsus loved spending time before the Blessed Sacrament. Today, if possible, go to a church or chapel and pray before the Blessed Sacrament. However, Saint Alphonsus, ever practical, realizing that it may not always be possible to make a visit to the Blessed Sacrament, wrote this spiritual communion. Pray it now:

My Jesus, I believe that you are in the Blessed Sacrament. I love you more than anything in the world, and I hunger to feed on your flesh. But since I cannot receive Communion at this moment, feed my soul at least spiritually. I unite myself to you now as I do when I actually receive you. Never let me drift away from you. Amen.

DAY 13

Praying for a Lively Faith

*I*n order to contemplate with tenderness and love the birth of Jesus, we must pray to the Lord for a lively faith.

THE INCARNATION, BIRTH AND INFANCY OF JESUS CHRIST

SCRIPTURE

[Thus says the Lord:] You, Bethlehem-Ephrathah, least among the clans of Judah, from you shall come forth for me one who is to be ruler in Israel; whose origin is from of old, from ancient times. Therefore the Lord will give them up, until the time when she who is to give birth has borne, then the rest of his kindred shall return to the children of Israel.

He shall take his place as shepherd by the strength of the LORD, by the majestic name of the LORD, his God; and they shall dwell securely, for now his greatness shall reach to the ends of the earth: he shall be peace.

MICAH 5:1–4A

PRAYER

O God, the holy Word instructs me to "wait on the Lord and be of good courage." In this Advent season of waiting, I admit I find it difficult to wait. Help me be patient with myself and with others. Allow me to slow down during this Advent season and to trust that with waiting comes unexpected blessings and wonderful opportunities to grow closer to you. I continue my Advent journey, believing you are with me to bring me to a place where your glory will be made known. Amen.

ADVENT ACTION

Today, take time to be quiet and listen to your inner self and seek God's will for your life.

DAY 14

Humility Stands Firm

We should always, even to the very last moments of our life, question our own strength and place all our confidence in God, always begging Him to give us humility.

THE PRACTICE OF THE LOVE OF JESUS CHRIST

SCRIPTURE

If there is any encouragement in Christ, any solace in love, any participation in the Spirit, any compassion and mercy, complete my joy by being of the same mind, with the same love, united in heart, thinking one thing. Do nothing out of selfishness or out of vainglory; rather, humbly regard others as more important than yourselves, each looking out not for his own interests, but [also] everyone for those of others.

PHILIPPIANS 2:1–4

PRAYER

God of power and mercy, open my heart in a spirit of welcome. Remove the things that hinder me from receiving Christ with joy so that I may share in Christ's wisdom and become one with him when he comes in glory. Amen.

ADVENT ACTION

At the end of this day, look for at least one blessing that has happened to you, and in a spirit of humility, offer a prayer of thanksgiving.

DAY 15

Our Mother Mary

*S*aint Bernardine of Siena tells us this: "The Blessed Virgin, by her consent to the Son's Incarnation, with the most intense ardor sought and obtained the salvation of all. By this consent she dedicated herself to the salvation of all. So much so that ever since, she has carried us in her womb as a true mother carries the children of her flesh."

THE GLORIES OF MARY

SCRIPTURE

Mary set out and traveled to the hill country in haste to a town of Judah, where she entered the house of Zechariah and greeted Elizabeth. When Elizabeth heard Mary's greeting, the infant leaped in her womb, and Elizabeth, filled with the holy Spirit, cried out in a loud voice and said, "Most blessed are you among women, and blessed is the fruit of your womb. And how does this happen to me, that the mother of my Lord should come to me? For at the moment the sound of your greeting reached my ears, the infant in my womb leaped for joy. Blessed are you who believed that what was spoken to you by the Lord would be fulfilled."

LUKE 1:39–45

PRAYER

Lord, I praise you because of your wonderful and marvelous deeds. You chose Mary to be the Mother of the Savior and through her brought salvation to the world. Having received Christ, like Mary, I too must make Jesus present to all those I encounter. Help me to continue to be joyful in knowing, loving, and serving the Savior. May all whom I encounter this day encounter Christ in me. Let me joyfully proclaim the Good News today, especially to those who may be depressed, mourning, or unhappy. Through me may they know that Emmanuel, "God with us," is in their midst. Amen.

ACTION ADVENT

Like Mary, visit someone today. Either visit or call a friend you have not spoken to in a long time and simply encourage them.

DAY 16

What Jesus Has Done for Us

*G*od has not only given you so much beauty and so many wondrous creatures in this world, he has also given you himself.
He "gave himself up for us" (Eph 5:2). Sin robs you of divine grace
and exposes you to eternal death. But the Son of God came on earth
to redeem you from that horrible fate and gain for you the grace of
eternal happiness.

PREPARATION FOR DEATH

SCRIPTURE

*Have among yourselves the same attitude that is also yours in
Christ Jesus, who, though he was in the form of God, did not
regard equality with God something to be grasped. Rather, he*

emptied himself, taking the form of a slave, coming in human likeness; and found human in appearance, he humbled himself, becoming obedient to death, even death on a cross.

Because of this, God greatly exalted him and bestowed on him the name that is above every name, that at the name of Jesus every knee should bend, of those in heaven and on earth and under the earth, and every tongue confess that Jesus Christ is Lord, to the glory of God the Father.

PHILIPPIANS 2:5–11

PRAYER

God, I stand in perfect obedience to your will. It is my desire to be used by you, to be a witness to the world of your Son, Jesus the Christ. I pray you will give me the anointing and the strength to bring others to you. I pray that at the name of Jesus every knee bend and every tongue confess that he is Lord. May my witness give you all the glory, honor, and praise. Amen.

ADVENT ACTION

On this day, take a look at something in your behavior or attitude that might be stopping your spiritual growth. It might be bitterness, holding a grudge, harboring jealousy, or spreading gossip. Determine how you will address the problem so you can experience the joy of the Lord in your life again.

DAY 17

We Must Love God

*O*nce your heart is detached from creatures, divine love immediately fills it. The human heart cannot live without love, so we must either love the Creator or creatures. If it does not love creatures, it *must* love God; so we must leave all to gain All!

THE PRACTICE OF THE LOVE OF JESUS CHRIST

SCRIPTURE

No one can serve two masters. He will either hate one and love the other, or be devoted to one and despise the other. You cannot serve God and mammon.

MATTHEW 6:24

PRAYER

Loving God, Jesus demonstrated the art of servitude. If I am to follow in his footsteps, then I also must adopt a posture of service to others rather than a posture in which I expect others to serve me. Please inspire me to see how I can live a life of service. May my sacrifice help others come closer to you. Help me gain an understanding of the life of Christ and his nature of service. You are the Creator of all things. You brought all things into being. In you we live and move and have our being. Lord, I pray you fill me with joy in serving others. Let my service not be for show, form, or fashion to this world, but to please you and you alone. Amen.

ADVENT ACTION

On this day, turn your attention to a friend, a relative, or a stranger who is struggling and see what you can do to help that person.

DAY 18

Playing the Role of the Beggar

*I*f we want to persevere in the grace of God until death, we must play the role of the beggar and ask for God's help. We should always repeat: "My Jesus mercy. Let me never be separated from You. O Lord, come to my aid. My God, help me." And we must remember this especially when we are severely tempted.

THE PRACTICE OF THE LOVE OF JESUS CHRIST

SCRIPTURE

At once the Spirit drove him out into the desert, and he remained in the desert for forty days, tempted by Satan. He was among wild beasts, and the angels ministered to him.

MARK 1:12–13

PRAYER

Beloved Jesus Christ: my Lord, my King, and my Savior. You who are God, but also was man, who was tempted by the devil as any other human being, please give me the strength to reject sin and the grace to remain as spotless as you are. Reign in my heart with your power, wisdom, love, peace, grace, purity, mercy, glory, and joy. Amen.

ADVENT ACTION

Today, turn your trials, temptations, and adversities over to God, and leave them with God. Trust that God really knows just how much you can bear.

DAY 19

Yearn Only for God

*M*y God, give me the courage to live for you alone, to love what you love. Let me die for you as you died for me. I deeply regret the times I have so selfishly ignored you. O will of God, I love you because you are one with God. I put myself at your command. You are my Love!

VISITS TO THE MOST BLESSED SACRAMENT

AND THE BLESSED VIRGIN MARY

SCRIPTURE

Seek the LORD while he may be found, call him while he is near. Let the wicked forsake their way, and sinners their thoughts; let him turn to the LORD to find mercy; to our God, who is generous in forgiving. For my thoughts are not your thoughts, nor are your ways my ways—oracle of the LORD. For as the heavens are higher than the earth, so are my ways higher than your ways, my thoughts higher than your thoughts.

Yet just as from the heavens the rain and snow come down and do not return there till they have watered the earth, making it fertile and fruitful, giving seed to the one who sows and bread to the one who eats, so shall my word be that goes forth from my mouth; it shall not return to me empty, but shall do what pleases me, achieving the end for which I sent it.

ISAIAH 55:6–11

PRAYER

Lord, I seek you while you may be found. I call on you while you are ever so near. Please, Lord, help and keep me day by day to live in a meek and humble way. I want to one day live with you in a mansion not made by hands. Lord, guide me day by day in a pure and perfect way. I want to one day live with you in a mansion not made by hands. Lord, encourage me and give me the grace to continue to run this race. I want to one day live with you in a mansion not made by hands. Amen.

ADVENT ACTION

Today, have an "attitude of gratitude." Remember a time when someone did something kind and considerate for you. Imagine receiving that act of kindness with open arms and grace. Pray for the health and well-being of that special person who showed you love.

DAY 20

"What I Am Before God, I Am"

*I*n order to grow in the love of Jesus Christ, then, we must learn to still the ambitions of self-esteem. And, until we do, we may never become true servants of Jesus Christ.

THE PRACTICE OF THE LOVE OF JESUS CHRIST

SCRIPTURE

[Beloved:] See what love the Father has bestowed on us that we may be called the children of God. Yet so we are. The reason the world does not know us is that it did not know him. Beloved, we are God's children now; what we shall be has not yet been revealed. We do know that when it is revealed we shall be like him, for we shall see him as he is.

1 JOHN 3:1–2

PRAYER

Thank you, Lord, for changing me from who I was to who I am. By your grace through faith, I am a new creation in Christ Jesus. I bless your holy name, that in accepting you as the Savior of my soul, my sinful condition is not my conclusion. You are a loving and redeeming God. As a child of God, I live in liberty, and I am truly thankful. Amen.

ADVENT ACTION

Advent is a season of change. It is a time of penance and seeking a deeper relationship with God. On this day, take time to review your life. Make an examination of conscience; see what, if any, changes should be made.

DAY 21

Extravagant Love

*B*oundless are your perfections, my Lord, and boundless is your love! Never let me appear again in the ranks of the ungrateful. Make me your tireless lover. I used to grow weary in your presence because my love was so weak. But your powerful grace can fan my love into a blazing fire. Then I will never tire of being at your feet.

VISITS TO THE MOST BLESSED SACRAMENT

AND THE BLESSED VIRGIN MARY

SCRIPTURE

Arise! Shine, for your light has come, the glory of the LORD has dawned upon you. Though darkness covers the earth, and thick clouds, the peoples, upon you the LORD will dawn, and over you his glory will be seen. Nations shall walk by your light, kings by the radiance of your dawning.

Raise your eyes and look about; they all gather and come to you—your sons from afar, your daughters in the arms of their nurses. Then you shall see and be radiant, your heart shall throb and overflow. For the riches of the sea shall be poured out before you, the wealth of nations shall come to you. Caravans of camels shall cover you, dromedaries of Midian and Ephah; all from Sheba shall come bearing gold and frankincense, and heralding the praises of the LORD.

ISAIAH 60:1–6

PRAYER

Gracious Savior, eternal Lord, I worship and adore you in this Advent season as the redeemer of my soul and the king of my heart. Your coming into this troubled and disturbed world of sin brought new hope to all humanity. Take full possession of my life, and may my thoughts and actions be acceptable and pleasing to you. Help me prepare a proper place for you to enter into my life. Come, Lord Jesus, and do not delay! Amen.

ADVENT ACTION

Advent is an appropriate time to turn back to God and to make amends for the times you have offended God. If you have not experienced the sacrament of reconciliation recently, make an appointment to be reconciled with God by doing penance and receiving absolution for your sins.

DAY 22

All Things Work for the Good

*E*ven past sins can contribute to our holiness because the memory of them keeps us more humble and more grateful, and because they help us to realize the favors God showers on us, even after we have offended Him.

THE PRACTICE OF THE LOVE OF JESUS CHRIST

SCRIPTURE

We know that all things work for good for those who love God, who are called according to his purpose. For those he foreknew he also predestined to be conformed to the image of his Son, so that he might be the firstborn among many brothers. And those he predestined he also called; and those he called he also justified; and those he justified he also glorified.

ROMANS 8:28–30

PRAYER

Lord, deliver me from the bondage of deception, lies, falsehoods, philosophical fallacies, practical blunders, and even from my own limited thinking. Lead me to a place of promise where truth and understanding abound. Lord, I desire to live a holy life. Help me to learn from and reverse my mistakes. Enable me to see and accept the good in all things. Let me acknowledge that just because I make mistakes, I'm not a mistake. Just because I fail doesn't mean I'm a failure. Just because I may be in a mess, I am not a mess. Lord, I seek to live for you. May you be glorified in my life. Amen.

ADVENT ACTION

On this day, if you have become angry at something or someone, acknowledge your anger, then let it dissipate and strive to restore peace within yourself or with the person who caused your anger. In the spirit of Saint Alphonsus, rid your life of anything that prevents you from becoming a saint.

DAY 23

The Gift of Faith

*R*emember that God has given all these resources to you without any merit or love on your part, and even with the foreknowledge of your own failure to love him as fully as he deserves. For when God thought of creating you and of giving you all these graces, he foresaw that at times you would fail to love him as you should.

PREPARATION FOR DEATH

SCRIPTURE

I give thanks to my God always on your account for the grace of God bestowed on you in Christ Jesus, that in him you were enriched in every way, with all discourse and all knowledge, as the testimony to Christ was confirmed among you, so that you are not lacking in any spiritual gift as you wait for the revelation of our Lord Jesus Christ. He will keep you firm to the end, irreproachable on the day of our Lord Jesus [Christ]. God is faithful, and by him you were called to fellowship with his Son, Jesus Christ our Lord.

1 CORINTHIANS 1:4–9

PRAYER

Loving God, I understand that where there is no vision, people perish. I thank you for the insight and the blessed assurance of a better day and a brighter tomorrow. Thank you for giving my life meaning and purpose, for calling me into divine fellowship with you. O God, you are so faithful to your covenant relationship with me. Help me to be faithful. Amen.

ADVENT ACTION

Take a long walk today and appreciate the beauty and wonder of God's creation and the precious gift of God's grace.

DAY 24

A Hope That Soars

*H*ope increases charity and charity increases hope, because hope in God's goodness undoubtedly helps us grow in love for Jesus Christ.

THE PRACTICE OF THE LOVE OF JESUS CHRIST

SCRIPTURE

[Beloved:] The grace of God has appeared, saving all and training us to reject godless ways and worldly desires and to live temperately, justly, and devoutly in this age, as we await the blessed hope, the appearance of the glory of the great God and

of our savior Jesus Christ, who gave himself for us to deliver us from all lawlessness and to cleanse for himself a people as his own, eager to do what is good.

But when the kindness and generous love of God our savior appeared, not because of any righteous deeds we had done but because of his mercy, he saved us through the bath of rebirth and renewal by the holy Spirit, whom he richly poured out on us through Jesus Christ our savior, so that we might be justified by his grace and become heirs in hope of eternal life.

TITUS 2:11–14; 3:4–7

PRAYER

Lord, you are coming and will not delay. I want to whole-heartedly trust in you. Release me from my doubt and despair. Banish my fears and wipe away my tears so that I may seek you and your kingdom above all other things. Help me to hope in you and increase my faith. I ask this in Jesus' name. Amen.

ADVENT ACTION

Saint Alphonsus reminds us that hope enables us to trust and love Jesus. It is also important to share the hope you have in Christ with others. Today, do something nice for a colleague or a loved one, or call or write a "thank-you" note to someone who has been a blessing in your life. Remember, "Hope increases charity."

DAY 25

Becoming Little to Make Us Great

*T*he Son of God has made himself little, in order to make us great. He has given himself to us, in order that we may give ourselves to him. He has come to show us his love, in order that we may respond to it by giving him ours.

THE INCARNATION, BIRTH AND INFANCY OF JESUS CHRIST

SCRIPTURE

Praise the LORD, for he is good; for his mercy endures forever;
Praise the God of gods; for his mercy endures forever; praise the
Lord of lords; for his mercy endures forever;

 Who alone has done great wonders, for his mercy endures
forever; who skillfully made the heavens, for his mercy endures

forever; who spread the earth upon the waters, for his mercy endures forever; who made the great lights, for his mercy endures forever; the sun to rule the day, for his mercy endures forever; the moon and stars to rule the night, for his mercy endures forever…
Praise the God of heaven, for his mercy endures forever.

PSALM 136:1–9, 26

PRAYER

Incarnate One, grant that your peace and love be rooted in my heart now freed from sin and be manifest in my concern for all the needs and worries of others. Through my witness may your love endure forever. Amen.

ADVENT ACTION

The Advent season encourages the Church to prepare to receive the greatest gift God could have given us: his Son, Jesus. God's love for the world was the impetus of this wonderful gift. And yet, even though God has already given us his most precious gift, there are those who feel abandoned, marginalized, disenfranchised, oppressed, and unloved. Today, do at least one concrete thing to help someone who is poor and needy, feels alone and unloved, or experiences pain and alienation.

DAY 26

All We See Is Love

You are a hidden God. These words of holy Scripture can be referred to Christ hidden in the Blessed Sacrament.

VISITS TO THE MOST BLESSED SACRAMENT

AND TO THE BLESSED VIRGIN MARY

SCRIPTURE

Where can I go from your spirit? From your presence, where can I flee? If I ascend to the heavens, you are there; if I lie down in Sheol, there you are. If I take the wings of dawn and dwell beyond the sea, even there your hand guides me, your right hand holds me fast. If I say, "Surely darkness shall hide me, and night shall be my light"—Darkness is not dark for you, and night shines as the day. Darkness and light are but one.

PSALM 139:7–12

PRAYER

O God, you made me and you know all about me. I cannot hide myself from you. If I were to go to the top of the mountain, you would be there. If I were to go to the depths of the valley, you would be there also. God, I come to you, acknowledging that I am like a sheep gone astray. I have failed to honor you in the ways I have lived my life. Have mercy, Lord. Enable me to live according to your way and not my own. Amen.

ADVENT ACTION

Today, make an effort to be aware of "a prayer need" in the world, your country, or community by reading the newspaper, watching a newscast on television or online, or listening to a radio news program. Focus on a certain situation that needs your prayers, your presence, and/or your commitment of service.

God Is Ready and Willing

*L*et us, therefore, receive him with affection. Let us love him, and present to him all our needs. "A child gives easily," says Saint Bernard; children readily give anything that is asked of them. Jesus came into the world as a child in order to show himself ready and willing to give us all good gifts: "The Father has given all things to him."

THE INCARNATION, BIRTH AND INFANCY OF JESUS CHRIST

SCRIPTURE

> *The word of the LORD came to me: Before I formed you in the womb I knew you, before you were born I dedicated you, a prophet to the nations I appointed you....*

But you, prepare yourself; stand up and tell them all that I command you. Do not be terrified on account of them, or I will terrify you before them; for I am the one who today makes you a fortified city, a pillar of iron, a wall of bronze, against the whole land: against Judah's kings and princes, its priests and the people of the land. They will fight against you, but not prevail over you, for I am with you to deliver you—oracle of the LORD.

JEREMIAH 1:4–5, 17–19

PRAYER

Lord, give me an open heart to listen and a willing spirit to respond. It is my desire to love you as you deserve to be loved. Your prophets, Jeremiah and Isaiah, announced that people will come from the ends of the earth to acclaim the Savior's presence. Help me listen to these new and surprising voices that teach me your ways, O Lord. Amen.

ADVENT ACTION

The lives of the saints inspired and motivated Saint Alphonsus. He constantly quoted them in his writings. Today, follow Saint Alphonsus' example and "spend some time with a saint" by reading a brief life of a saint and try to put into practice a virtue or characteristic of that saint.

DAY 28

God Whom We Behold as a Child

esus has chosen to come as a little Child to make us love him,
not only with an appreciative but even a tender love.

THE INCARNATION,
BIRTH AND INFANCY OF JESUS CHRIST

SCRIPTURE

The people who walked in darkness have seen a great light; upon those who lived in a land of gloom a light has shone. You have brought them abundant joy and great rejoicing: they rejoice before you as people rejoice at harvest, as they exult when dividing the spoils. For the yoke that burdened them, the pole on their shoulder, the rod of their taskmaster, you have smashed, as on the day of Midian. For every boot that tramped in battle, every cloak rolled in blood, will be burned as fuel for fire.

For a child is born to us, a son is given to us; upon his shoulder dominion rests. They name him Wonder-Counselor, God-Hero, Father-Forever, Prince of Peace. His dominion is vast and forever peaceful, upon David's throne, and over his kingdom, which he confirms and sustains by judgment and justice, both now and forever. The zeal of the LORD of hosts will do this!

ISAIAH 9:1–6

PRAYER

O Christ, radiant dawn, splendor of eternal light, sun of justice, shine on me, illumine the dark places of my life, and give warmth to my sometimes cold heart. Break my routine of indifference and selfishness with the splendor of your freedom. I feel your presence. I anticipate your coming. I acknowledge your majesty. Let the waiting be over! Come, Lord Jesus, I need Emmanuel! I need God to be with me and with the world. Amen.

ADVENT ACTION

Today is Christmas Eve, and you are at the threshold of the commemoration and celebration of the birth of Jesus Christ. What joy and excitement you must feel at this long-anticipated moment! At the end of this Advent sojourn and the beginning of the Christmas season, take some time to think about your purpose in life. Do you feel productive? Fulfilled? Consider one thing you can do today to make your life more spiritually meaningful, and then do it! Consider this to be a special Christmas gift to yourself.

PART II

~

READINGS

for the

CHRISTMAS

SEASON

DAY 1

He Came Down From Heaven

*T*he birth of Jesus Christ is truly a cause for universal joy. He is the Redeemer, the one whose coming had been looked for, and sighed for, throughout all the centuries of the Old Testament. It was there that he was called the desired of the nations, of the everlasting hills. And now he has finally come into this world: born as an infant in a stable, a shelter for animals.

A CHRISTMAS NOVENA

SCRIPTURE

In those days a decree went out from Caesar Augustus that the whole world should be enrolled. This was the first enrollment, when Quirinius was governor of Syria. So all went to be enrolled, each to his own town. And Joseph too went up from Galilee from the town of Nazareth to Judea, to the city of David that is called Bethlehem, because he was of the house and family of David, to be enrolled with Mary, his betrothed, who was with child. While they were there, the time came for her to have her child, and she gave birth to her firstborn son. She wrapped him in swaddling clothes and laid him in a manger, because there was no room for them in the inn.

LUKE 2:1–7

PRAYER

Incarnate God, bright and morning star, Word made flesh who now dwells among us: your grace has appeared, bringing salvation to the world. While I have waited for this blessed hope, today is the manifestation of your abundant and abounding love for me. Though I am a sinner, you loved me and sent Jesus to be born, just to die for my sins and the sins of the whole world! I love you. May my love offering in gratitude for the greatest love of all, Jesus, spread the compassion, the healing, and the work of justice that Christ's coming has announced and his ministry has proclaimed. Amen.

CHRISTMAS ACTION

Merry Christmas! On this day that you celebrate the wonderful God-given gift of the Incarnation, may Jesus bless your life abundantly with love, peace, joy, health, and happiness. At the end of this day, after the gifts have been exchanged, the festive Christmas meal enjoyed, and family and friends have returned home, take a few minutes to yourself and enjoy a special gift from Saint Alphonsus. Meditate on his famous Christmas hymn, *"Tu Scendi Dalle Stelle, O Re del Cielo"* ("You Come Down From the Stars, O King of Heaven").

(ENGLISH VERSION)

O King of Heaven! from starry throne descending,
Thou takest refuge in that wretched cave:
O God of bliss! I see Thee cold and trembling.
What pain it cost Thee fallen man to save!

Thou, of a thousand worlds the great Creator,
Dost now the pain of cold and want endure;
Thy poverty but makes Thee more endearing,
For well I know 'tis love has made Thee poor.

I see Thee leave Thy Heavenly Father's bosom,
But whither has Thy love transported Thee?
Upon a little straw I see Thee lying;
Why suffer thus? 'Tis all for love of me.

But if it is Thy will for me to suffer,
And by these sufferings my heart to move,
Wherefore, my Jesus, do I see Thee weeping?
'Tis not for pain Thou weepest, but for love.

Thou weepest thus to see me so ungrateful;
My sins have pierced Thee to the very core;
I once despised Thy love, but now I love Thee,
I love but Thee; then, Jesus, weep no more.

Thou sleepest, Lord, but Thy heart ever watches,
No slumber can a heart so loving take;
But tell me, darling Child, of what Thou thinkest.
"I think," he says, "of dying for Thy sake."

Is it for me that Thou dost think of dying!
What, then, O Jesus! can I but love Thee?
Mary, my hope! If I love him too little—
Be not indignant—love him thou for me.

DAY 2

The Reason He Was Born

Some people, upon reading the story of the presentation of Jesus in the Temple, might wish to have the same privilege that the aged Simeon had, that of holding the child Jesus in his arms. We should remember, however, that when we receive Holy Communion, the same Jesus who was born in Bethlehem is present not only in our arms but in our very selves. This is why he was born, to give himself entirely to us. "For a child has been born for us, a son given to us" (Isaiah 9:5).

A CHRISTMAS NOVENA

SCRIPTURE

Now there was a man in Jerusalem whose name was Simeon. This man was righteous and devout, awaiting the consolation of Israel, and the holy Spirit was upon him. It had been revealed to him by the holy Spirit that he should not see death before he had seen the Messiah of the Lord. He came in the Spirit into the temple; and when the parents brought in the child Jesus to perform the custom of the law in regard to him, he took him into his arms and blessed God, saying:

"Now, Master, you may let your servant go in peace, according to your word, for my eyes have seen your salvation, which you prepared in sight of all the peoples, a light for revelation to the Gentiles, and glory for your people Israel."

LUKE 2:25–32

PRAYER

God, your goodness and kindness have appeared to us in Jesus Christ. Your holy Child has put on human flesh and moved into our human community. Like Simeon, my eyes have waited to gaze upon the Child born in Bethlehem. Let the radiant light of your glory sweep upon my heart. Forgive my sins. Remove all that is unpleasing to you. Make my life a worthy sanctuary to receive you. One day, I wish to say with Simeon, "Now, Master, you may let your servant go in peace, according to your word, for my eyes have seen your salvation, which you prepared in sight of all the peoples, a light for revelation to the Gentiles, and glory for your people Israel." Amen.

CHRISTMAS ACTION

As the Christ Child was presented in the Temple, "present" yourself to someone who really needs your time and your undivided attention. Your presence may be something someone really needs and has long awaited. Be sure to spend time actively listening to this person God has placed before you at this moment. Pass no judgment on what they are sharing with you; simply be present to them.

DAY 3

Mary and Joseph: Pilgrims on the Way

*I*magine, if you will, the many devout and holy conversations which Joseph and Mary had on the way to Bethlehem. How they must have dwelt on the mercy, the goodness, the love of their God whose Son was so soon to appear on earth for the salvation of the human race! Listen in your mind to the words of praise and benediction, the acts of thanksgiving and humility and love, which these two holy pilgrims must have recited along the way.

A CHRISTMAS NOVENA

SCRIPTURE

And Mary said: "My soul proclaims the greatness of the Lord; my spirit rejoices in God my savior. For he has looked upon his handmaid's lowliness; behold, from now on will all ages call me blessed. The Mighty One has done great things for me, and holy is his name. His mercy is from age to age to those who fear him. He has shown might with his arm, dispersed the arrogant of mind and heart. He has thrown down the rulers from their thrones but lifted up the lowly. The hungry he has filled with good things; the rich he has sent away empty. He has helped Israel his servant, remembering his mercy, according to his promise to our fathers, to Abraham and to his descendants forever."

LUKE 1:46–55

PRAYER

Blessed Savior, Mary and Joseph gave their all and followed the divine plan as foretold by the angel. What courage! What obedience! I pray for the courage and humility in this Christmas season to seek and follow God's divine plan for my life. Lord, help me to put aside all my desires and distractions and to follow where you lead me. Lord, I trust you. Lord, I desire your will for my life. Amen.

CHRISTMAS ACTION

Do something for a colleague, friend, acquaintance, or family member. Buy that person a cup of coffee, treat him or her to lunch, compliment him or her on the day's choice of apparel, or simply express happiness that he or she is part of your life.

DAY 4

Whom Shall I Love?

I know that in the past I have grieved you by my sins, but since you have come to seek me, I throw myself at your feet. And even though I see you humbled and afflicted on a manger bed in Bethlehem, I acknowledge you as my Lord and my God. I feel that your infant cries and your baby tears invite me to love you; they demand my heart. Behold it, then, my Jesus, I offer it to you today. Change it and inflame it with holy love for you.

A CHRISTMAS NOVENA

SCRIPTURE

O God, you are my God—it is you I seek! For you my body yearns; for you my soul thirsts, in a land parched, lifeless, and without water. I look to you in the sanctuary to see your power and glory. For your love is better than life; my lips shall ever praise you!

PSALM 63:2–4

PRAYER

Glory to God in the highest and on earth, peace! Thank you, amazing God, for giving us eternal life in Jesus Christ. Christmas day has come and gone. The gifts have been exchanged and the wrapping paper thrown away, and yet I still marvel and praise you for the awesome Christmas story! Homeless parents, with no food, friends, or family around, are forced to have their Child in a stable, filled with animals and awful smells. The Child of Peace is laid in a manger, signifying that he is food for the hungry, the Bread of Life for a starving world. Today, O God, let the joy that shone in the face of Baby Jesus and the tenderness of his countenance be in me. Today, may I be a living witness to the glory of the Lord that the angels sang about in Bethlehem so long ago. Amen.

CHRISTMAS ACTION

On this day, pray for peace in our world. Pray for an end to all adversity, hatred, and prejudice, which divides the Body of Christ.

A Suffering Child

*C*onsider the great sorrow and deep distress that must have filled the heart of the Infant Jesus when, in the very first moments of his existence in his mother's womb, his Eternal Father revealed to him all the contempt, the agony, and the many sufferings he was going to suffer on earth in order to save us from the punishments due to sin.

Thus it is proper to say that all that Jesus was to suffer during his life and especially in his death was made known to him while he was in Mary's womb. And at the same time it is equally true to say that he accepted it all with delight, somehow overcoming the natural repugnance of the senses to suffering, but still feeling in his innocent heart the deepest anguish and oppression.

A CHRISTMAS NOVENA

SCRIPTURE

[Beloved:] Remember Jesus Christ, raised from the dead, a descendant of David: such is my gospel, for which I am suffering, even to the point of chains, like a criminal. But the word of God is not chained. Therefore, I bear with everything for the sake of those who are chosen, so that they too may obtain the salvation that is in Christ Jesus, together with eternal glory. This saying is trustworthy:

If we have died with him we shall also live with him; if we persevere we shall also reign with him. But if we deny him he will deny us. If we are unfaithful he remains faithful, for he cannot deny himself.

2 TIMOTHY 2:8–13

PRAYER

Newborn King, reign in my heart this day. I love you, dear Jesus, and yet I confess at times my hesitation to identify with you because of my own insecurities and malice. Forgive my sinful inclinations. Let your grace and forgiveness touch me, cleanse me, and help me to see you more clearly and love you, myself, and others more dearly. Amen.

CHRISTMAS ACTION

In appreciation for the "Word made flesh" who now dwells among us, spend some time today reading the Bible or a spiritual book.

DAY 6

Desire of the Nations

*C*onsider that, after so many centuries of waiting, after so many prayers and sighs of longing, the Messiah finally arrived. He whom the holy patriarchs and prophets were not worthy to see, he who was the desire of the nations, "the desire of the eternal hills," came into the world. He was born into the world, and gave himself entirely to us: "A child has been born for us, a son given to us."

A CHRISTMAS NOVENA

Scripture

The LORD is king; let the earth rejoice; let the many islands be glad.…

The heavens proclaim his justice; all peoples see his glory.…

Light dawns for the just, and gladness for the honest of heart. Rejoice in the LORD, you just, and give thanks at the remembrance of his holiness.

PSALM 97:1, 6, 11–12

Prayer

O my Jesus, is it true that You came down from heaven to make me love You? Is it true also that You embraced a life of suffering and death on the cross for my sake? Is it true that You did this in order that I might welcome You into my heart, and yet I have so often driven You away by my sins? O dear God, if You were not infinite goodness, if You had not given up Your life for me, I would never have the courage to ask for pardon. But I feel that You offer me pardon and peace: "Return to me, says the LORD of hosts, and I will return to you" (Zech 1:3).

You, O Lord, have made Yourself our intercessor. "If anyone does sin, we have an Advocate with the Father, Jesus Christ, the righteous one; and he is the atoning sacrifice for our sins" (1 Jn 2:1–2). I will not insult You again by not trusting in Your mercy. I repent with all my heart for having offended You, and with Your grace I will never drive You away again by sin.

Mary, my Queen and my Mother, pray to Jesus for me; make me live the rest of my days in this world grateful to the God who has loved me so much, even after I have so greatly offended him. Amen."

SAINT ALPHONSUS LIGUORI

CHRISTMAS ACTION

Today is a new day. No matter how content you may be with your routine, try something new, whether it means substituting tea for coffee or taking a new route to work or speaking with someone you may not know very well. In trying something new, may you also come to experience God's grace and mercy that is new each day.

DAY 7

A Journey of Trust

*J*oseph, we are sure, was himself ready to undergo whatever sufferings and pain were an essential part of the journey. These were, he felt, also a part of the Eternal Father's plan for his own Son in achieving our salvation....They were poor, and as Saint Bernard has written, Joseph had to work day and night to feed and support his family, a family that contained one member who alone provides food for all people of the earth!

MEDITATIONS IN HONOR OF SAINT JOSEPH

SCRIPTURE

When they had departed, behold, the angel of the Lord appeared to Joseph in a dream and said, "Rise, take the child and his mother, flee to Egypt, and stay there until I tell you. Herod is going to search for the child to destroy him. Joseph rose and took the child and his mother by night and departed for Egypt. He stayed there until the death of Herod, that what the Lord had said through the prophet might be fulfilled, "Out of Egypt I called my son."

MATTHEW 2:13–15

PRAYER

Eternal God of epiphanies and redeeming God of revelations, enable us to lift up our eyes and look around; the glory of the Lord shines all around. Your light gives me the ability to see and thus to confess my need for you. Your light causes me to look inward to change and not outward to blame others. Your light pulls me up to action instead of down in hopelessness. Your light means transformation, new life, new hope, and new joy. Lord, let me walk in your light and be a gift of light to those who continue to hide in the darkness. Amen.

CHRISTMAS ACTION

Jesus was certainly grateful for Joseph and Mary in his life. On this day meditate on your parents or on the adults who have been guardians or parent figures to you. Thank God for the spiritual nourishment, the moments of encouragement, and even the correction they gave you. Today, offer a prayer of gratitude for your parents or guardians and for the gift of life.

DAY 8

Jesus Enlightens Us

*I*f then we wish for light, Jesus has come to enlighten us. If we wish for strength to overcome our enemies, Jesus has come to give us peace and security. If we wish for pardon and salvation, Jesus has come to forgive and save us. If indeed we wish for the greatest gift of all, divine love, Jesus has come to fill and inflame our hearts with this grace.

A CHRISTMAS NOVENA

SCRIPTURE

The angel said to them, "Do not be afraid; for behold, I proclaim to you good news of great joy that will be for all the people. For today in the city of David a savior has been born for you who is Messiah and Lord.

LUKE 2:10–11

PRAYER

Gracious God, may the celebration of the birth of your Son restore your Church and enable it to bring healing, deliverance, and encouragement to your people. I ask you this through "the One" you have sent us and for whom I wait, Christ the Lord. Amen.

CHRISTMAS ACTION

On this day, think about people who have helped you, encouraged you, alleviated your fears, prayed you through some difficult times; someone who proclaimed to you some "good news." Offer a prayer for someone who prayed for you when you were in need of prayer.

DAY 9

The Father's Will

*J*esus was fully human so without a doubt he naturally felt repugnance at the thought of suffering and of dying, especially
the kind of death so painful and full of shame as he was destined to
experience. But at the same time he was able to understand perfectly
and accept totally the Father's will, even though this meant that he
would begin from that moment on to suffer, at least interiorly, the
anguish and pains of his crucifixion and death.

A CHRISTMAS NOVENA

SCRIPTURE

Do not store up for yourselves treasures on earth, where moth and decay destroy, and thieves break in and steal. But store up treasures in heaven, where neither moth nor decay destroy, nor thieves break in and steal. For where your treasure is, there also will your heart be.

MATTHEW 6:19–21

PRAYER

Redeemer Lord, I admit that sometimes my focus is not on you. I am shamefully wooed by worldly distractions. My heart is far from you. I have learned from my past transgressions and indiscretions that you are the one and only source of my peace and security. Lord, I give up on you too easily. Please grant me the grace of perseverance. I desire your will over my life. Please help me, Jesus. Amen.

CHRISTMAS ACTION

Saint Alphonsus insisted his Redemptorist missionaries take an oath of perseverance. He knew well that anything worthwhile would demand diligence and the fortitude to face life's challenges. What are some struggles that frustrate you that you wish you could simply give up? Write them down, and pray for the grace of perseverance.

DAY 10

God's Love Is Eternal

*I*f in the past we have shut our eyes to the light, not remembering the love Jesus has shown for us, let us during the time left to us on earth try to meditate often on the suffering and death of Jesus, our Redeemer. If we do this, then we will perhaps come to love him very much, but never as much as he has loved us.

A CHRISTMAS NOVENA

SCRIPTURE

"And this will be a sign for you: you will find an infant wrapped in swaddling clothes and lying in a manger." And suddenly there was a multitude of the heavenly host with the angel, praising God and saying: "Glory to God in the highest and on earth peace to those on whom his favor rests."

LUKE 2:12–14

PRAYER

By the long-awaited coming of your newborn Son, deliver me, Lord, from the expectations of others. Rid me of my judgmental inclinations. Free me from pride, and lead me into the simplicity of knowing and believing in others. And then, dear God, enable me to love others as you love them. I ask this through Christ our Lord. Amen.

CHRISTMAS ACTION

Because you have seen the light and you have an enduring relationship with Jesus, take a moment today to rededicate yourself to the vision and tenacity it takes to create a better place and space within your church community now and for future generations.

No Room for Ingratitude

*I*f in the past we have spoken so ungratefully to our loving God, does that mean we must continue to do so? Not at all, for our loving Savior in no way deserves our ingratitude. He came down from heaven to suffer and die for us; now we must love him in return.

A CHRISTMAS NOVENA

SCRIPTURE

Exalt him before every living being, because he is your Lord, and he is your God, our Father and God forever and ever! He will afflict you for your iniquities, but will have mercy on all of you. He will gather you from all the nations among whom you have been scattered. When you turn back to him with all your heart, and with all your soul to do what is right before him, then he will turn to you, and will hide his face from you no longer.

Now consider what he has done for you, and give thanks with full voice. Bless the Lord of righteousness, and exalt the King of the ages.

TOBIT 13:4–6

PRAYER

Almighty God, the birth of your Son has come. It is my humble prayer that your eternal Word, who took flesh in the womb of the Virgin Mary and came to dwell among us, will show the world the greatness of his love and mercy. He lives and reigns with you and the Holy Spirit, God forever and ever. Amen.

CHRISTMAS ACTION

Saint Alphonsus vowed never to waste a moment of time. Today, avoid procrastination. Do not put off until tomorrow what you can do today. If it has been a while since you've told Jesus you loved him, do it today. If it has been some time since you expressed gratitude to the One who was born so you might have eternal life, do it today. Live your life fully and productively as a way of praising God for the very gift of life.

DAY 12

Blessed Hope

The words of Scripture encourage us to do this "while we wait for the blessed hope and the manifestation of the glory of our great God and Savior, Jesus Christ" (Tit 2:13). We may await with hope, for the Father has promised us the paradise which Jesus has won for us by his life and death on earth.

A CHRISTMAS NOVENA

SCRIPTURE

[Christ Jesus] is the image of the invisible God, the firstborn of all creation. For in him were created all things in heaven and on earth, the visible and the invisible, whether thrones or dominions or principalities or powers; all things were created through him and for him. He is before all things, and in him all things hold together. He is the head of the body, the church. He is the beginning, the firstborn from the dead, that in all things he himself might be preeminent. For in him all the fullness was pleased to dwell, and through him to reconcile all things for him, making peace by the blood of his cross [through him], whether those on earth or those in heaven.

COLOSSIANS 1:15–20

PRAYER

Loving God, thank you for the precious gift of your Son, Jesus. I graciously receive Jesus into my life. Let me not keep silent in a world that needs to hear a prophetic voice. Give utterance to my words, O Lord, that I might be a witness to your holy name. Fill my heart with joy and love until my actions speak louder than words. Let those around me see you in me. As I go through my everyday duties, I pray not to forget you. May there be opportunities each day for me to share my knowledge and love for you, witnessing to your abundant love, mercy, hope, and will. Lord, you are my inspiration. Please guide my life so that in happy moments, I will praise you; in difficult moments, I will seek you; in quiet moments, I will worship you; in painful moments, I will trust you; and in every moment of life and living, I will thank you. Amen.

CHRISTMAS ACTION

Perhaps today as the Christmas season ends, you can demonstrate your love and devotion to the newborn King by volunteering in your community, sending a note card to cheer up an elderly relative living alone, or taking a bag of bakery cookies to a recently widowed neighbor. Whatever you choose to do today, do it from the heart and with no expectation of receiving anything in return.

PART III

~~~

FORMATS
for
NIGHTLY
PRAYER
and
READING

Formats for Nightly Prayer and Reading

THE PURPOSE OF PRESENTING two optional formats for nightly reading and prayer is to offer ways to use the material in this book for group or individual prayer. Of course, there are other ways in which to use this book—for example, as a meditative daily reader or as a guide for a prayer journal—but the following familiar liturgical formats provide a structure that can be used in a variety of contexts.

FORMAT 1

OPENING PRAYER

The observance begins with these words:

God, come to my assistance.
Lord, make haste to help me.

followed by:

Glory to the Father, and to the Son,
and to the Holy Spirit, as it was in the beginning,
is now, and will be for ever. Amen. Alleluia.

EXAMINATION OF CONSCIENCE

If this observance is being prayed individually, an examination of conscience may be included. Here is a short examination of conscience; you may, of course, use your own preferred method.

1. Place yourself in a quiet frame of mind.

2. Review your life since your last confession.

3. Reflect on the Ten Commandments and any sins against these commandments.

4. Reflect on the words of the gospel, especially Jesus' commandment to love your neighbor as yourself.

5. Ask yourself these questions: Have I been unkind in thoughts, words, and actions? Am I refusing to forgive anyone? Do I despise any group or person? Am I a prisoner of fear, anxiety, worry, guilt, inferiority, or hatred of myself?

PENITENTIAL RITE (OPTIONAL)

If a group of people are praying in unison, a penitential rite from the *Roman Missal* may be used:

Presider: You were sent to heal the contrite of heart:
Lord, have mercy.

All: Lord, have mercy.

Presider: You came to call sinners:
Christ, have mercy.

All: Christ, have mercy.

Presider: You are seated at the right hand of the Father to intercede for us:
Lord, have mercy.

All: Lord, have mercy.

Presider: May almighty God have mercy on us,
forgive us our sins,
and bring us to everlasting life.

All: Amen.

HYMN: "O COME, O COME, EMMANUEL"

A hymn is now sung or recited. This Advent hymn is a paraphrase of the great "O" Antiphons, written in the twelfth century and translated by John Mason Neale in 1852.

O come, O come, Emmanuel,
And ransom captive Israel;
That mourns in lonely exile here,
Until the Son of God appear.

Refrain: Rejoice! Rejoice! O Israel,
         To thee shall come Emmanuel!

O come, thou wisdom, from on high,
And order all things far and nigh;
To us the path of knowledge show,
And teach us in her ways to go. (*Refrain*)

O come, O come, thou Lord of might,
Who to thy tribes on Sinai's height
In ancient times did give the law,
In cloud, and majesty, and awe. (*Refrain*)

O come, thou rod of Jesse's stem,
From ev'ry foe deliver them
That trust thy mighty power to save,
And give them vict'ry o'er the grave. (*Refrain*)

O come, thou key of David, come,
And open wide our heav'nly home,
Make safe the way that leads on high,
That we no more have cause to sigh. (*Refrain*)

O come, thou Dayspring from on high,
And cheer us by thy drawing nigh;
Disperse the gloomy clouds of night
And death's dark shadow put to flight. (*Refrain*)

O come, Desire of nations, bind
In one the hearts of all mankind;
Bid every strife and quarrel cease
And fill the world with heaven's peace. (*Refrain*)

PSALM 27:7–14—GOD STANDS BY US IN DANGERS

Hear my voice, LORD, when I call;
    have mercy on me and answer me.
"Come," says my heart, "seek his face";
    your face, LORD, do I seek!
Do not hide your face from me;
    do not repel your servant in anger.
You are my salvation; do not cast me off;
    do not forsake me, God my savior!
Even if my father and mother forsake me,
    the LORD will take me in.

LORD, show me your way;
    lead me on a level path
    because of my enemies.
Do not abandon me to the desire of my foes;
    malicious and lying witnesses have risen
        against me.
I believe I shall enjoy the LORD'S goodness
    in the land of the living.
Wait for the LORD, take courage;
    be stouthearted, wait for the LORD!

RESPONSE

I long to see your face, O Lord. You are my light and my help.
Do not turn away from me.

SCRIPTURE READING

Read silently or have a presider proclaim the Scripture of the day that is selected.

RESPONSE

Come and set us free, Lord God of power and might. Let your face shine on us and we will be saved.

Glory to the Father, and to the Son,
and to the Holy Spirit:
as it was in the beginning, is now,
and will be for ever. Amen.

SECOND READING

Read silently or have a presider read the words of Saint Alphonsus Liguori for the day selected.

CANTICLE OF SIMEON

Lord, now you let your servant go in peace;
    your word has been fulfilled:
my own eyes have seen the salvation
    which you have prepared in the sight of every people:
a light to reveal you to the nations
    and the glory of your people Israel.

Glory to the Father, and to the Son, and to the Holy Spirit:
as it was in the beginning, is now,
and will be for ever. Amen.

PRAYER

Recite the prayer that follows the excerpt from Saint Alphonsus Liguori for the day selected.

BLESSING

May the all-powerful Lord grant us a restful night and a peaceful death. Amen.

MARIAN ANTIPHON

Loving mother of the Redeemer,
gate of heaven, star of the sea,
assist your people who have fallen yet strive to rise again.
To the wonderment of nature you bore your Creator,
yet remained a virgin after as before.
You who received Gabriel's joyful greeting,
have pity on us poor sinners.

FORMAT 2

OPENING PRAYER

The observance begins with these words:

God, come to my assistance.
Lord, make haste to help me.

followed by:

Glory to the Father, and to the Son,
and to the Holy Spirit, as it was in the beginning,
is now, and will be for ever. Amen. Alleluia.

EXAMINATION OF CONSCIENCE

If this observance is being prayed individually, an examination of conscience may be included. Here is a short examination of conscience; you may, of course, use your own preferred method.

1. Place yourself in a quiet frame of mind.

2. Review your life since your last confession.

3. Reflect on the Ten Commandments and any sins against these commandments.

4. Reflect on the words of the gospel, especially Jesus' commandment to love your neighbor as yourself.

5. Ask yourself these questions: Have I been unkind in thoughts, words, and actions? Am I refusing to forgive anyone? Do I despise any group or person? Am I a prisoner of fear, anxiety, worry, guilt, inferiority, or hatred of myself?

PENITENTIAL RITE (OPTIONAL)

If a group of people are praying in unison, a penitential rite from the *Roman Missal* may be used:

All: I confess to almighty God
and to you, my brothers and sisters,
that I have greatly sinned,
in my thoughts and in my words,
in what I have done and in what I have failed to do,

And, striking their breast, they say:
through my fault, through my fault,
through my most grievous fault;

Then they continue:
therefore I ask blessed Mary ever-Virgin,
all the Angels and Saints,
and you, my brothers and sisters,
to pray for me to the Lord our God.

Presider: May almighty God have mercy on us,
forgive us our sins,
and bring us to everlasting life.

All: Amen.

Hymn: "Behold, a Rose"

A hymn is now sung or recited. This traditional hymn was composed in German in the fifteenth century. It is sung to the melody of the familiar "Lo, How a Rose E're Blooming."

Behold, a rose of Judah
From tender branch has sprung,
From Jesse's lineage coming,
As men of old have sung.
It came a flower bright
Amid the cold of winter
When half spent was the night.

Isaiah has foretold it
In words of promise sure,
And Mary's arms enfold it,
A virgin meek and pure.
Through God's eternal will
She bore for men a savior
At midnight calm and still.

Psalm 40:2–8—Thanksgiving for Deliverance

Surely, I wait for the LORD;
  who bends down to me and hears my cry,
Draws me up from the pit of destruction,
  out of the muddy clay,
Sets my feet upon rock,
  steadies my steps,

And puts a new song in my mouth,
  a hymn to our God.
Many shall look on in fear,
  and they shall trust in the LORD.

Blessed the man who sets
his security in the LORD,
  who turns not to the arrogant
  or to those who stray after falsehood.
You, yes you, O LORD, my God,
  have done many wondrous deeds!
And in your plans for us
  there is none to equal you.
Should I wish to declare or tell them,
  too many are they to recount.

Sacrifice and offering you do not want;
  you opened my ears.
Holocaust and sin-offering you do not request;
  so I said, "See; I come
  with an inscribed scroll written upon me.
I delight to do your will, my God;
  your law is in my inner being!"

RESPONSE

May all who seek after you be glad in the Lord, may those
who find your salvation say with continuous praise, "Great
is the Lord!"

SCRIPTURE READING

Read silently or have a presider proclaim the Scripture of the day that is selected.

RESPONSE

Lord, you who were made obedient unto death, teach us to always do the Father's will so that, sanctified by the holy obedience that joins us to your sacrifice, we can count on your immense love in times of sorrow.

Glory to the Father, and to the Son,
and to the Holy Spirit:
as it was in the beginning, is now,
and will be for ever. Amen.

SECOND READING

Read silently or have a presider read the words of Saint Alphonsus Liguori for the day selected.

Canticle of Simeon

Lord, now you let your servant go in peace;
    your word has been fulfilled:
my own eyes have seen the salvation
    which you have prepared in the sight of every people:
a light to reveal you to the nations
    and the glory of your people Israel.

Glory to the Father, and to the Son,
and to the Holy Spirit:
as it was in the beginning, is now,
and will be for ever. Amen.

Prayer

Recite the prayer that follows the excerpt from Saint Alphonsus Liguori for the day selected.

Blessing

Lord, give our bodies restful sleep and let the work we have done today bear fruit in eternal life. Watch over us as we rest in your peace. Amen.

MARIAN ANTIPHON

Hail, holy Queen, mother of mercy,
>   our life, our sweetness, and our hope.
To you do we cry,
>   poor banished children of Eve.
To you do we send up our sighs,
>   mourning and weeping in this vale of tears.
Turn then, most gracious advocate,
>   your eyes of mercy toward us,
>   and after this exile
>   show to us the blessed fruit of your womb, Jesus.
O clement, O loving,
O sweet Virgin Mary. Amen.

Sources and Acknowledgments

WORKS OF SAINT ALPHONSUS LIGUORI

From the Heart of Saint Alphonsus: Excerpts From Saint Alphonsus Liguori, edited by Norman J. Muckerman, CSsR (Liguori, MO: Liguori Publications). Copyright © 2002 by Norman J. Muckerman. Used with permission.

Preparation for Death: Prayers and Consolations for the Final Journey, Excerpts From Saint Alphonsus Liguori, edited by Norman J. Muckerman, CSsR (Liguori, MO: Liguori Publications). Copyright © 1998 by Norman J. Muckerman. Used with permission.

Selected Writings and Prayers of Saint Alphonsus (A Liguori Classic), adapted for Modern Readers by John Steingraeber, CSsR (Liguori, MO: Liguori Publications). Copyright © 1997 by Liguori Publications. Used with permission.

The Glories of Mary by Saint Alphonsus Maria de Liguori (A Liguori Classic). (Liguori, MO: Liguori Publications) Revised edition copyright © 2000 by Liguori Publications. First edition copyright © 1962, 1963 by Redemptorist Fathers of New York. Used with permission.